Nothing's Lost

Ian House taught in England, the United States, Moscow, Budapest and Prague. His first collection, *Cutting the Quick*, was published by Two Rivers Press in 2005. He lives in Reading.

By the same author:
Cutting the Quick, Two Rivers Press (2005)

Also by Two Rivers Poets:
Paul Bavister, *The Prawn Season* (2002)
Kate Behrens, *The Beholder* (2012)
Adrian Blamires, *The Effect of Coastal Processes* (2005)
Adrian Blamires, *The Pang Valley* (2010)
Joseph Butler, *Hearthstone* (2006)
Terry Cree, *Fruit* (2014)
Jane Draycott, *Tideway* (2002)
Claire Dyer, *Eleven Rooms* (2013)
John Froy, *Eggshell: A Decorator's Notes* (2007)
David Greenslade, *Zeus Amoeba* (2009)
A. F. Harrold, *Logic and the Heart* (2004)
A. F. Harrold, *Postcards from the Hedgehog* (2007)
A. F. Harrold, *Flood* (2009)
A. F. Harrold, *The Point of Inconvenience* (2013)
Ian House, *Cutting the Quick* (2005)
Gill Learner, *The Agister's Experiment* (2011)
Kate Noakes, *The Wall Menders* (2009)
Tom Phillips, *Recreation Ground* (2012)
Victoria Pugh, *Mrs Marvellous* (2008)
Peter Robinson, *English Nettles and Other Poems* (2010)
Peter Robinson (ed.), *Reading Poetry: An Anthology* (2011)
Peter Robinson (ed.), *A Mutual Friend: Poems for Charles Dickens* (2012)
Lesley Saunders, *Her Leafy Eye* (2009)
Lesley Saunders, *Cloud Camera* (2012)
Susan Utting, *Houses Without Walls* (2006)
Susan Utting, *Fair's Fair* (2012)
Jean Watkins, *Scrimshaw* (2013)

Nothing's Lost

Ian House

First published in the UK in 2014 by Two Rivers Press
7 Denmark Road, Reading RG1 5PA.
www.tworiverspress.com

© Ian House 2014

The right of the poet to be identified as the author of the work
has been asserted by him in accordance with the Copyright,
Designs and Patents Act of 1988.

All rights reserved. No part of this publication may be reproduced,
stored in or introduced into a retrieval system, or transmitted,
in any form, or by any means (electronic, mechanical, photocopying,
recording or otherwise) without the prior written permission of
the publisher.

ISBN 978-1-909747-00-5

1 2 3 4 5 6 7 8 9

Two Rivers Press is represented in the UK by Inpress Ltd and
distributed by Central Books.

Cover design and illustration by Sally Castle.
Text design by Nadja Guggi and typeset in Janson and Parisine.

Printed and bound in Great Britain by Imprint Digital, Exeter.

Acknowledgements
My thanks to the many people who have encouraged me and
criticised my poems; to Adrian Blamires and Lawrence Sail for their
detailed suggestions about the whole collection; and to Susan Utting
for her continuing advice and support.
   Some of these poems first appeared in the Creative Arts
Anthologies of Reading University, *Reading Poetry* (Two Rivers
Press, 2011) and *Sitegeist*.

Contents

Peregrine | 1
On Fire | 2
Discovering Cows | 3
Light and Shade | 5
Silver Bream | 6
Masterstroke | 8
Aldeburgh: Samain | 9
Uprush | 10
A Day in the Sun | 11
The Open Door | 12
Takeover | 13
Georgian Wineglass | 14
Still Life with Oranges and Walnuts | 15
Incarnation | 16
One for the Birds | 17
The Boar's Head | 18
Time and Relative Dimensions in Space | 19
Looking at Morandi | 20
No End To It | 21
Stove | 22
Gaunt | 23
Frontage | 24
Real Estate | 25
Mother | 26
Wanted | 27
Here and Now | 28
There and Then | 30
How We Are | 31
Revision | 32
The Ring | 33
Crushed Velvet | 34
Making Up | 35
Looking for Myself | 36
My On-Off Affair with Anxiety | 37
1 a.m. | 38
Nightfall | 39
At Large | 40

Somewhere in Moscow | 41
If It Ever Started | 42
Bystander | 43
Gogol on the Loose | 44
Boris Aleksyeevich Trigorin | 45
Slow Fade | 46
Electroplate | 47

Peregrine

She floats to hand, hooks to the leather fist
like that other self he sees in the mirror,
inches from his eyeballs and a world away.

His craft and will against her flint,
her slate feathers, notched beak,
coalpit eyes. He works her
with hoodwink and lure.

Nothing's gentler than the manning
as he smooths her head with a feather,
nothing's more delicate
than the two-tone tinkle of bells
as she glides to a treetop.

He feels, far back,
how his hand balanced a spear,
how his belly warmed
to the ribbon of blood.

Whatever it is that rises from the long grass
at two hundred yards is dead already.
Her stoop shears the sky,
pure and inhuman as Aldebaran.

Not for her the hawk's swerve
to the tossed gobbet. She'll biff
a rook like a bullet, grab and rip
like a machine, strip life
to the bone, like poetry.

He thrills to that truthfulness,
its cold, transparent tarn; longs
for her life of pounce and gorge,
of lazing and killing; worships
one untrammelled by love or pity.

On Fire

Well, yes, I admired the chutzpah and adroitness
with which you angled your glasses
and drew the sky's blaze to a pinpoint

and the care in the crinkling of paper,
the nesting of kindling,
the judgement of coals
which had brought you to your knees

but what is this fitful, banked fire
to the flare of poppies, to maple leaves
or a ladybird's wing-case? Last week,

in the bleached arboretum, a dazzle
of winterberries on invisible twigs,
crimson stars in their thousands

and just today, by the local shops, a fox.
We paused: two animals, alert, respectful.
Then he trotted, dainty-footed, unhurried,
into shadow, his brush erect
and tipped with the fierce sunrise.

Discovering Cows

Cows were splotched, flaky, thumb-high, tin.
Redcoats raided the farmyard, gorged on beef.

China ornaments in a distant field; nearer,
black-and-white maps. They wobbled
like the fat woman at the end of the road.
Their bellies sagged and swayed,
their bagpipes were swollen and pink.
Their pats steamed, repulsive, fascinating,
and hardened into volcanic rocks.

'They give us cheese, butter, leather, meat.
In India they are holy. In Alpine valleys
tinkling bells are heard for miles. They are
ruminants, ungulates and quadrupeds.'
Words thick and juicy as flesh.

Strange to think they have names: Fancy looks scraggy;
Buttercup's the cream of summer, stored;
Daisy should be nimble as a hornpipe.
A youngster slaps their rumps and guides them home.

One balances on a shelving bank, drinking.
She is massive and dainty, a ton
perched on four spindles that pick their way.
Her tail conducts a zestful orchestra.

Tess rests her cheek on a smooth flank.
Hands tug teats hard as carrots. We listen
as milk squirts and purrs into the pail.

I trample the grass with my alien smells,
belong to a tribe that has marked them for death.
All I can see in their eyes is reproach.

Hands round earthenware bowls
of warm, unpasteurized milk.
Home-baked bread. Hearts appeased.

Cuyp's sunlight gilds a flank. Four of them:
standing or at rest, they are monumental, equable,
share the world for the present with the milkmaid,
her bucket, a windmill, two passing birds.
They live through aeons.

Some thirty block the river bank.
I sidle through: an animal from another herd.
A hoof might lash, panic ripple.
If one shifts its weight, I'll be crushed.
They are solid, rooted, warm.

Light and Shade

At first I took them for sculptures:
on one bank the angler
studious over his rod,
his eye on the float,
on the other an unruffled
wedding-guest, a young heron

but stood long enough
to see the man rub his thumb
on the rod's cork handle,
try a sandwich, pick up another,
scratch his nape,
glance at the seething gentles

while the heron was stone-still
but for repetitive, mechanical head-flicks.
Millions of years had pared
the dagger bill, the repertoire.
I wanted his yellow searchlight eye,
his stillness before lightning

then thought: better a brilliant, cleared sky
or clouds and their nuances?

Silver Bream

How sexy bream are,
industrious lap dancers
in slinky chainmail,
silverleaf bodystockings,
always, always on the move:
mouth, muscles, gills and fins.

The Blind Watchmaker,
patient as Dürer,
tiled these flanks,
dropped each granulated
blob of solder into place.

In this nanomachinery
the eye is a hulking washer,
the pupil a black hole.

There is sadness in fish,
in the tearable flesh
of the mouth and the gills.

Look long enough,
one becomes a friend,
a little old man, pursing
and puffing his thick lips.
Is his speechlessness
empty-headed or wise?
His world's laid bare
but he's as other
as angels or trilobites.

The tank's Grand Central:
each fish, driven by hunger
on its course, defers to each.
The patterns are traceless
strolls in a watery park.
If there were souls,
they'd dance like this
to a wandering flute,
octaves beyond us.

Masterstroke

Your feet follow the dips and bends
of the towpath or the lie of the grass.
Rushes are bent into huts and hairdos,
catkins flirt in the breeze.

A coot snails upstream
on a diagonal, half-drifting,
half fighting the current
so its bill misses nothing.

The wind teases a flickering
network of light from the water
to a boat's white bow:
a galaxy forming and fading.

The oarsman, headed wherever,
inscribing the watery steppe,
looks for eddies and snags,
for advantages. Water submits

to muscle and will, to the robotic pull
of the blades, the swift scissors
till on the bend, as he feathers,
stilled, poised in his shell,

he's the keystone that locks into one
clouds, willows, water-birds, river.

Aldeburgh: Samain

To stand at the sea's edge
at the lip of the mouth of sea and sky
with your back to the known world
is to lose all thought
of the sink and chink of pebbles,
the waffle-print of shoes on sand,
the pisspot tinkle of rigging,
the ravel of netting and creels,
improbably scarlet valerian:
all, now, fainter than a smoke-smudge
on the horizon, a gull's cry,
and lost in the ocean's elisions.
You are baffled and soothed.

The sky gives itself to the sea
as purple-brown moorland, pink gashes,
an ink stain, a knife-edge of sunlight
and drains to luminous pearl
as the mind flickers, foam-like,
and settles; it settles, it sways,
is one with the sea's indifference,
with the salt tide coursing the body,
scouring, unassuageable.

The sea returns and returns
you to yourself, rucking and unrucking;
it heaves and expires. Gravestones topple,
leave lines of old men's dribble at your feet.
Someone howls like a dog.
It is the wind. It's you.

Uprush

All winter it was slate:
the scratch of clumsy runes,
fractiousness, the burin's skid.
Slate. The word slithers and hardens.

Now my mind cleaves and lightens
to the pink and purple and turquoise
of the sea's shuffling mosaic,
the exuberant swell
of its running longhand,
the iambic tide in the blood.

On the ocean floor, at the hot gates,
there is a welter of microbes,
spongy jungles, spectral crabs

and, in clear water, a butterfly ballet
of flickering damselfish
and the improbably brilliant yellow
of blue-girdled angels.

A Day in the Sun

In and out of a pearly rumple
of bedclothes-clouds
the sun pinged a roof slate,
zebra-striped the river.
Stepping-stones, hatched with gold,
were Galapagos tortoises, a field
was a crystallographer's lattice.

We swam in sunlight,
the wash of plastered walls,
a flood
everywhere and invisible, known
only as it pulsed from things.
We bathed in equanimity,
warmth unfastened us.
If one believed in God, now…

We drank light,
drowned in it,
wanted to bottle it,
watch it thicken to primroses,
to a greenfinch's olives and yellows,
a goldfinch's startle of red.

Under a cloudless sky (the sun
beyond ferocity, pitilessness)
things were themselves
– barn, beech tree, boulder –
speakable only as by-products
of hydrogen fusing to helium.

A late sun painted the world.
It hammered leaves to bronze
and fired the pyracantha. Clouds
were tie-dyed crimson and indigo.

The Open Door

'One minute there's whatever – an apple,
a cow, a wall of crizzled bricks,
a cardboard box with gaping flaps –
and the next, no longer instrumental, familiar,
they are – how to put it? – themselves,
and I'm dumbed by wonder at simply their being,
at the worth of it all. It's not the mind's lurch
from blackberries to ink spots. Rather,
it's the silent hour we watched the beetle
trekking the infinite floor. Remember how
in his last years Jack's face was lit,
each spring, by flowers he'd never seen,
the purple crocuses?' I struggled on. Smiling,
she pointed to Fox Talbot's photograph
of a besom propped at an open door,
the incidence of light on twigs and stones.

Takeover

Mind, you're a table,
knotted, oak-hard, right-angled,

wanting, you tell me,
to be like the freesias'
open-handed petals
shading from off-white to lilac.

Damn you, look at this table, look
at its spoor of cuts, stains, botches,
maps, isobars, hanging bats,
bogs, sand spits, flukes of light;

look till it's chiaroscuro,
till everything's table,
till the table's unreal
like a word spoken too often,
till it's dissolved and become you.

Draught-blown, the freesias are dancing,
loud-mouthed in the sun.

Georgian Wineglass

Sand and fire,
fusion's rage,
split-second gather and blow,
swing and spin of the pipe.

A slip of a thing,
water and air,
mizzle-coloured,
breath visible.

The eye loiters
from foot to stem
to flaring trumpet,
skates the rim.

The one tear is for
its unbearable beauty,
the pontil's hidden
unavoidable scar.

Still Life with Oranges and Walnuts

Someone's left on the table
nine oranges, two earthenware jugs,
a dish of walnuts, a melon,
a four-hooped cask
and a scatter of boxes

making, for the mind,
against a wall of black,
an austere geometry
of rectangles, cylinders and spheres
behind the intractable walnuts

while the eye is warmed
by the jugs' terracotta,
sunlit wood,
lamps of orange,
the melon's fine striations.

The nested fruit and grainy shells,
the splintery, pitted wood,
these rough ceramics,
once man-handled and half-seen,
are solid, incontrovertible.

It took Meléndez a lifetime
to arrange this happy accident,
a table containing this-and-that,
a translation into paint so scrupulous
that how things are, it seems, they have to be.

Luis Meléndez (1716–80)

Incarnation

Coptic textile, c. AD 300 (Musée des Tissus, Lyon)

I

Some kind of perch maybe, monsters,
gold-flanked, with crimson fins –
not fins but manes or tattered sails.
The shoal hurtles through the twilit museum,
a projectile of hunger. Once hyper-real,
pure kitsch. Now faded, threadbared,
each fish is the weft of its flash
through the water, the warp of its flesh.

II

Hoard the murex's thin secretions,
the stigmas of saffron. Grind madder.
Wash flax, card wool. Throw the shuttle,
pattern the scales and bars of a fish,
a delicate gill, each ray of a fin. Let time
strip its body to the shape of need,
its mouth to a gape.

III

Had the weaver seen these fish,
ragged and ravenous,
he'd have glimpsed his Christ.

One for the Birds

Straight out of Pliny, I grant you,
but true nonetheless:

I was in Room 30 of the National Gallery
last Wednesday, when a pigeon walked in

on finicky toes, flicking her button eyes
from sour Martha to slumped Christ to John

seeing things on the Island of Patmos.
She too saw what she wanted:

a cup of water. I loved
the solid, canvas-coloured cup,

the glisten of light on the rim,
the sliver of limpid water, symbolizing—

so I'd read—the Virgin's purity.
The pigeon rose like a delighted child,

chivvied the water with her beak, and departed
on derisive, whistling wings.

The Boar's Head

It's no more than a hunk of limestone
sheathed in lead, gilded, tusked,
with a mouth like pink blancmange:
Cerberus at the gate of a cemetery
of stuffed animals, cracked pots, bygones.

It seems like yesterday he thrust himself
from the tile-hung wall of a squat alehouse
and I saw his hackles bristle
and the jeweller's, auctioneers' and wool shop
dissolve into woodland as he snouted
for beech mast, birds' eggs, mice.

He was descended from Trwyth,
who laid waste one-third of Dyfed,
from whose jaws ran the blood of a thousand chickens,
whose tusks ripped the bellies of a cry of hounds
until Arthur's men *laid hold of his feet*
and soused him in Severn.

You'll see him in the border of a Book of Hours
between a knot and two crossed, flaming sticks:
life in the fierceness of being,
in thought's interlacements.

He thunders into the land of the dead.
I follow. We rootle together.

The Boar's Head guards the entrance to Reading Museum.

Time and Relative Dimensions in Space

Once the Tardis has materialised
under the sequoia on the lawn
of Oxford's Pitt Rivers Museum
you shrink through the door
and your neck is yanked
up the helter-skelter backbones
of iguanodons and pterosaurs
into the light-filled Gothic vault.
Here is the armature of an anorexic
velociraptor, slashing the air
with its sickle. Here
are meteorites and tektites,
milky, glowing selenite,
flecked granite, basalt turds.
Here is a giant ammonite,
coiled like a ship's cable,
adrift in time like that witless
pigeon in Mauritius at which,
as it flapped down the beach,
the sailors took potshots.

Among the lutes and masks,
the baskets and the charms,
in glass cases as strange
and intimate as your first kiss,
you enter the world of betel-chewing:
crushers and slicers, bamboo pots,
ivory boxes, dishes of massala,
teeth crusted with betel and lime,
dusty nouns to which you bring the verbs.

In 2001 Mark Wallinger installed a Tardis outside (and another (?) inside) this museum.

Looking at Morandi

When I see these pale flasks, bottles, jars
        at the edge of a table
a cityscape unchanging monumental

always now it's a Sunday one December
when a pane of glass, four foot square, wobbles,
starts – will it? – to fall
and my hand dithers
                and the pane's not 'frozen'
but simultaneously falling and receding
(a willed, hopeless re-winding)
in a moment that's no time at all
                and longer than lasting
till someone I find to be me
has his right hand clamped round the thumb of his left
which is ripped (almost off? to the bone?)
and senses already the unending sequelae
of stitches, infection, night nurses,
the weeks-long ebbing of purple and yellow
(compacted by memory to moments)

and a flask's in mid-air,
drenched in crimson.

Giorgio Morandi, Italian painter (1890–1964)

No End To It

These cups and saucers are that afternoon. 'Puce'
is the word for them: stoneware, lustrous, vitrified.
Beetles inhabit the pansies. A spoon has a moonface.
A bream floats in an oval bowl, an eye in its flank.

Mrs Mace. That was it: Mrs Mace.
She smelt of fish. Her nose was a gannet's beak.
I tasted the green bile in her mouth.
She had sat in this room, yammering,
for centuries. My parents drank the milky tea.
I refused a slice of poisoned cake,
counted and re-counted nineteen clocks
on dresser, table, cupboards, chest of drawers.

Time's face smirks from a platter.
A dish marks the hours from II to IV
and stops. Mrs Mace bites a lump from a plate
and crunches it with teeth as sharp
as the slop basin's sawtooth rim.

Claire Baker, ceramics, Barn Galleries, Aston, Henley-on-Thames, 2010.

Stove

There since the world began,
cast iron, cold, black.
Fat baked-in like resentment.

Its warmth eased the house.
We gathered to the smell of cloves,
roasts, rice puddings.
Grease warmed our bellies.

Stove. A hiss of gas, a click,
the mouth rounding,
closing on fur.

The door clanks open. Again
a leg glistens and spits.
The animal breath's on my face.

Gaunt

When I learnt the word, I'd known for years what it meant:
my dead, angular grandmother on the front-room wall,
a grey woman in a grey dress among grey hollyhocks,
grudging daylight. Was she throttling the cat?
Her right hand was a diagram in our *Family Doctor*,
her lips clenched like a mousetrap. This
was what mothers turned into. Sundays,
I imagined, she knelt in a cold church.
Mondays she scrubbed her men's collars. Tuesdays
she made rissoles from gristle. Under that eye
balloons were foolishness, rummy a sin.
Greyness hung in the kitchen, flowed up the stairs.
I was told later what flowered in her
unknown, that she never complained,
that the word for her hair was 'sparse'.

Frontage

Down two cracked steps, then fast
(shrinking to the wall of the passage)
by terraced one-storey houses
blistered and slipshod,
women frowsy as net curtains,
their children smelling of sardines,
to a weeping yard
little bigger than himself,
unable not to think of his grandmother
squatting in the privy.
Her kiss-soft, whiskery mouth.
Her witchy hump. How he loved her.
He brushed the backdoor lintel with his hair,
smelled fish before he smelled it.

Aunts smiled like pianos,
tinkled tea into gold-rimmed cups,
whispered about Cancer.
One winked at him, like a brass,
in the gaslight. The Father of All Cats,
easy as an uncle, stretched His claws
and revved up on the window ledge;
His shirt was always Sunday-white.
For all the blowing of the golden trumpeters,
the hands were fixed at ten to eight.
When he crept through the front door
and turned in head-high grass,
three storeys stared him down,
blank-eyed, with quizzing brows.

Real Estate

Mother, of course, was the iron (this was the fifties),
my brother, as you'd expect, the battleship
and I was the top hat, who slunk through Whitechapel,

where Jack spring-heeled from gas lamps to shadows,
past murderers gibbering and gobbing in Pentonville,
to stroll down Pall Mall, quizzing club bores and swells.

It was all joy: the clatter of bones, the held breath,
wads of orange and crimson and lilac,
unctuous Deeds. I'd seen

the pigeons in Trafalgar Square, the neon signs
for chewing-gum in Piccadilly Circus and I wanted
Bond Street (shoppers in tiaras) and Mayfair (paved with gold).

And Father? He was Banker and Lawgiver.
He talked about stocks and shares, return on capital.
I learnt that houses come and go, that Chance

could land you in Queer Street.
I can't walk now from the Angel to Park Lane
but Oxford Street's green, still, and Fleet Street red.

Mother

Nothing much to see, a house like any other
in this terrace between workhouse and board school:
brick, two-up, two-down. I hurried past
the fresh white door, the glittering windows,
yet smelt rotting meat in the kitchen and climbed
to a room in which someone must dream
of Mrs Dyer's slug-flesh face, soft eyelids,
smooth hands, long and tapering fingers.

Neighbours hardly knew they were puzzled
when babies entered that conjuror's box
and vanished. Mrs Dyer loved poetry,
found a thing to do, wound the edging tape
three times her little throat around
and jerked it. She let them die quickly.

It's more than a mile to the Thames.
My feet beat out the names:
Doris Marmon, Harry Simmons, Helena Fry.
The parcel grows heavier. She called herself Mother.

Amelia Elizabeth Dyer, baby farmer. Murdered at least thirty babies.
Last lived in Kensington Road, Reading. Hanged 1896

Wanted

*WANTED: Home for Baby Boy, age 1 month; complete surrender.
Write Box 173, Mercury, Reading. [1942]*

And when you'd passed the parcel, you heard
the ragged firing squad of slamming doors
and saw the jaunty handkerchiefs, the khaki men
leaning from windows to their dwindling sweethearts.

The line stretched, a cord of elastic, till it snapped
at the bend. And then the chill return
through Wokingham, Crowthorne and Sandhurst,
his milky breath, your hands' emptiness.

And down the years, as silence walled the house,
a thought like the flicker and rasp of grasses:
how your mind was always turning back,
how your feet had kept going.

Here and Now

I'm wishing I could be Frank O'Hara and stop for a cheeseburger and chocolate malted at JULIET'S CORNER and watch the girls' skirts blow up over grates and the Puerto Ricans stand about on the avenue

or Ginsberg deep in the watermelons and avocados and brilliant cans of a California supermarket

but there's nothing to do or to see because it's eleven o'clock on a morning in mid-January in Reading, England, and the sky's grey and the rain only just holding off and the wind gusting under the narrow sky

and in the purple-framed windows of Moonstone's Gifts and Crafts the salt lamps are tired and crystals hang dispiritedly and there's a plastic Gandalf

and opposite there's the vast dirty redbrick fortress of Brock Barracks and a public lavatory, boarded-up, and it's cold and I'm coughing in the wind and hurry past the Polish Delikatesy,

the halal meats, the Tabernacle of the God of Prophecy (once a bank), a benign Sikh, Caribbean Supreme Cuisine ('1 piece chicken + rice'), a line of rubbish bins throwing up, two smiling (Japanese?) girls in leggings, pink and orange

to peer in at Afro and European Human Hair where a woman hunts for a colour match among the plastic-sheathed scalpings hung round the walls.

The whole world's nested here: nose flutes, maracas, hypnotic tablas, notes scattered on the freezing wind; almost, when you listen, a symphony.

High over the hard and glittery porcelain of Bathroom Collection there's the faded elegant black lettering of Dunlop's Hay & Straw Factors and briefly wagons creak and horses drop steaming dung under the eyes of men with watch chains.

In fuggy Costa Coffee an old woman tells herself she wants a glass of hot lemon with sugar and asks an empty chair, 'Where did you go on holiday?' and blesses me with a smile.

Outside, a spaceship has landed and thrusts its gold antenna at the sky. And next to the mosque there's a sex shop's chaste windows.

Time now to catch the bus somewhere between the greengrocer's, where the sun lights, for a moment, on limes, Turkish peppers, guavas so that they gleam as if with little bulbs inside
   and House Clearance next door, the sediment and history of suffering, laughter, lives: sofas and paintings, dinner plates, board games, photo frames.

There and Then

Where I am, with a live wire's jolt,
when a man in whites tosses a ball
from one hand to the other isn't the Quad,
Monday morning, when we hung about,
silent, with lowered eyes

but where I'd not been that cloudless Saturday,
on the boundary, the pavilion clock at five past four
and shock-haired Jack Barnes tosses the ball
from hand to hand
                (as though a curtain goes up
on a scene still playing, fifty years on,
to its end)
          shuffles into his stride,
runs in with his head-down hurtle
and lets fly a ball that lands short,
flies up, thuds into Mr Rodd's chest.
He sways, drops the bat, falls.

Till then I'd known death by its traces:
the no-longer-thereness of those who'd been old,
a catch in a voice. Not how it comes for you,
out of the blue, unerring.

How We Are

It feels like the scuffle of a key
at what might be the wrong lock,
then slides home and I find,
in a cradle of plump cheeks,
her face at eighteen, a Meissen,
her rueful eyes (ah, yes, blue-grey!)
and, as my lips press soft, remembered flesh
(her ribs were warm beneath their skim of silk),
we're caught in an uprush,
a sparkle and spatter of waves
till our eyes flitter for clues, for scars
and we're left high and dry
to semaphore gauchely.

'Lovely to see you': the requiem chime.
She's replaced every cell in her body
but, as we turn to the rest of our lives
and she sways down the street,
she's dancing through a joss stick room
and I know, looking back, that I knew,
without knowing, that the girl
was the woman that she'd become.

Revision

I remember it as though it were yesterday,
I say, lying as usual. I can't even
remember her name, Ellen Something,

(was it Spanish she taught?), the cut of her hair,
what she wore. What happens again and again
in my head, what's happening twenty years on,

as I tell you, is how, at the end
of that first week, the two of us, newcomers,
passed at the turn of the stairs, and paused,

exhausted, emptied of selfhood. Our eyes
opened, sudden, helpless, into each other's
and we knew what we were, what we are

at the root: something impersonal, need.
In less than a second, far less than a second,
we'd bumped back to cream-washed walls,

our bags of books, walked away from each other,
unreeling the cord all these years. Her eyes,
as I make them out now, are the palest of blues.

The Ring

A dignified seal bobbed a beach ball,
a ladder swung the clown round and round.
A girl, gold hair scraped back,

green leotard cut to the crotch,
wheel-bound at wrists and ankles,
a V on an upturned V,

teeth bared for her glittering partner,
for the eyes that have paid to watch her,
is spinning as steel-beaked birds whiz

too close to her ears and toe-nails,
marking the line of her legs,
the arc of her head to the hair-line

until we're released from the blizzard of being
the thrower, the knives and the woman
as she tiptoes, thighs arched, across sawdust,

pirouettes, curtseys, forgives us.

Crushed Velvet

When he talked to the dresses she'd taken, his hands smoothed
   velvet, slid on silk.
He threw out the hangers, their sad shoulders. Like a photographic
   negative
absence made her real near a phantom table, the glimmer of a chair.
Even when he'd gone through the house, he came across a hairgrip,
her *Copper Fire* lipstick, a note at the back of a drawer. He dreamt
of a rubbish tip piled with her shopping bags and Simone de
   Beauvoir,
her copies of *Cosmo*, the ironic pink eggcup. He burnt what he
   could
and hammered the rest. One day, by the furrowing sea, his stick
wrote her name in the sand. He watched the tide swirl the grains
to wherever, because of the writing, they'd go. Though things
   smash
to smithereens and the fusions of memory, nothing's lost. They'd
   stood once
in a strange light in a flooded meadow as a white horse, leading her
   foal,
picked her way over a violet wash, hoof by high-stepping hoof.

Making Up

Do you remember the Chinese paintings we saw
in – where was it? Prague – vast fields of white
and how grey wisps, a smudge of blue
made mountains and rivers and waterfalls?
Today snow's stolen the world. Green's gone.
A smooth pelt's draped over everything:
dark matter made visible, a gravecloth.

How long must we wait till the eye is appeased
by the glow of the faintest of pinks, set off
by the glitter of particles? Do you remember
the head of that man, smooth as an egg,
we passed in a crowd: the lipless gap,
the lidless slits, two holes for nose?

Don't answer. Take my hand.

Looking for Myself

I've lost my glasses again and it's all there,
even the stars, but bigger and blurrier.
My neighbours' walls have no mortar courses,
their fences no slats. Trees fly perished sails,
roses are flames. Everyone I meet
is skin-deep, coloured smears, like late Monet.
I wave to strangers, feel forwards
through a fuzz of possibilities, am five
in early September at the playground's edge.
No straight lines in nature, people say,
and they're right. Everything frays
into everything else. Books on my shelves
are accordions of colour. As I sit at my desk,
a girl in green slacks, cherry sweater,
runs to me across a field near Chichester
in nineteen seventy-four and I'm straining
to make out her face, which dissolves
like the horizon where cloud fades to sea
and sea is a smear of cloud. I see myself,
jigsawed in shifting waters. Thoughts like deer
glimpsed in their swift passage through trees?
Like the spasms of disco dancers in strobe light?
Like particles' streaks in a cloud chamber.

My On-Off Affair with Anxiety

I wake and think I'm blind
before the torch throws Saturn
on the wall. Ah, you're flirting.

Your idea of a joke:
a phone call at midnight.

You wait in a roomful of strangers,
a crimson spot on the pillow,
the look in her eyes.

We've lived together for years
through syphilis and H-bombs,
melting ice-caps, pandemics.

If this were a poem and you were a bird,
you'd be a vulture, a jackdaw,
a repetitious parrot.
An animal? A scorpion.

Once it was take-offs and train-times,
zips stuck, a drawn curtain.
Now it's heartbeats, the future.

You like it rougher each day,
use itching veins, poems drying.
I can't remember what happens
in the novel I'm reading.

Straggle-haired crone! Prima donna!
I know what you're doing,
fixing my tongue to the swelling,
my mind to the speed of the poisons,
the morphine, my death-bed.
I divorce you. It's over.

What will my life be
without the frissons you've given ?

1 a.m.

She shivers at the taps of her heels down the boardwalk
past walls bleared by streetlights
to a door where she steps through shadows

to the gape of the yellowy armchair,
the panicky tree in the picture,
the moonbleached table.

She presses the fist of one hand
to the palm of the other
and knows she is living.

Nightfall

At age fourteen, he said,
he'd locked the bathroom,
cleaned his teeth,

looked into the mirror
and aimed the gun

into that other mouth.
We heard the starburst glass,

his sisters banging on the door,
a voice running the stairs

and saw the blue revolving light,
the shaking boy

and did not ask him why
but sipped our coffee,

watching the reflections
as the windows darkened
and the lamps blinked on.

At Large

So far today I've been a passport page
(photo, date of birth, three Given Names)
or spiralling half-truths for fellow passengers,

then a parcel hurtled from Sheremetevo
through miles of grey apartment blocks (an armed
guard in a café doorway, at a cinema *Titanic*) and now,

dumped, unpacked, I'm scattered round a room
as half-a-dozen shirts (familiar checks and stripes),
a can of shaving foam, a pile of underpants,

flotsam from Reading in a Moscow flat,
what's left when someone dies in hospital.

The tablecloth is Gran's, chenille and fringed
(but hers was green). In a mirror a grey-haired man
clings to Eliot (Faber, 18s 0d, yellow jacket, torn),

beside him an engraving of *Napoleon und Sein Sohn*,
a flaxen girl apparently. A shelf of medical text-books,
an angler's guide, Bunin and Sholokhov: I puzzle out

my landlord from Cyrillic like the window's ice ferns,
am conscious of my self as of a buzzing fly,
think of that drawing (whose was it?), the solidity

of the one rearing horse born from the sea
in a thousand self-cancelling chalk strokes.
I shall go out, find myself in the blizzard

among the onion domes and lit-up liquor stalls.

Somewhere in Moscow

She picks up a carrot and slices
the feathery green from the frost-blackened root.
There are hundreds to get through

and you know the street, brown with snow, crawls
for a mile and three-quarters, that they drop
in the pail like the minutes
and days of this featureless woman
wearing two rusty coats tied with string

and you want their rough skin in her hands
to bring back the marl round the dacha,
her mother's lace collar, the wink of a match
in the bowl of her grandfather's pipe,
the birch forests smaller than hope.

If It Ever Started

If it ever started, the clock on the wall has stopped.
If there were windows, it would be a fish tank.
The smell of sweat is a uniform, the horizon

a square of frosted glass in a door; two places gained
go to the head like champagne. Faces are smeared
by low-watt bulbs, by guilt calibrated like sickness:

the too-easy laugh, the hand smoothing the sleeve.
Histories are rehearsed silently, re-made
to accord with the bundle of papers each carries.

A slip of the tongue, you slither the length of the snake.
There is nothing he will not tell the priestess,
purple lipstick stamped on her face like his dream.

In a country yards away and in another time
men board trams, eat dumplings, laugh.

Bystander

Before long I was used to Stalin,
Yeltsin, Trotsky, three Lenins
smoking in the Metro corridor,
chatting up women in furs.
The Lenins were small fellows,
light on their feet, smirkers.
Uncle Joe, bear-friendly, sent millions
to the gulags, wore ropes of flowers,
dandled children, was only on Thursdays.
I'd throw roubles into their caps.

One day Hitler had joined them,
with his swastika armband,
pasty-faced, scowling. When he smiled,
the walls dizzied. How,
as he stuck on the ludicrous bristles,
he could look in his eyes
concerns me no more than that others
played Mozart. What worries me now
is that none of it worried me
till a cartoon of evil
solidified out of childhood.

Gogol on the Loose

They opened his coffin and found
what remained of him, supine,
claw marks on the lid's underside,
and remembered he'd been cataleptic.
Don't think of him waking, whispering,
of his eyes opening, re-opening,
of his fingers tracing the satin cocoon,
of the screams the owls heard.
                              Think of his nose,
that magnificent hooter, so long and droopy
his lower lip reached it. Picture that ripsnorting
nose as it floats through woodwork and soars
over squadrons of angels and generals
for one last sniffing-out of Moscow,
one last, delirious strafing
of apparatchiks and jobsworths,
of bureaucrats, bullionaires, lickspittles.
                                      Think
how that irrepressible and promiscuous nose
will weep for men at the back doors of restaurants,
for the woman who buys one tomato,
for the waitress who's dusting, leaf by leaf,
a plastic birch.
                    That piteous nose will drape
round the shoulders of Akaky Akakiyevich
as he squats in the lee of a monastery wall,
sucking the neck of a bottle, a new overcoat,
quilted, double-seamed, with silk-lined hood.

Boris Aleksyeevich Trigorin

Anton Chekhov, The Seagull

'A broken bottle, the neck of a broken bottle
glistening on the dam, the shadow of a mill-wheel ... '
A moonlit night: that's it! Who'd not be Trigorin,
writer, fisherman, rapt at the lakeside?
Such a charming philanderer, hair curled,
with his cream linen jacket, handkerchief flaring.
Yet helpless on the treadmills of writing and sex,
he pounces by reflex. He can't see a cloud
without scribbling 'snowdrift', 'piano',
and knows, as soon as it's written, it's wrong.

His teeth gleam in a spotlight. He's a pike
hovering in weeds for the hair-triggered dart
and strong-jawed snap. And the prey,
juggled and swivelled into the head-first,
mouth-splitting gulp isn't cloud or a girl.
He says he devours his life with his fictions.
He's a killing machine that's turned on itself.

Slow Fade

Not, now, even an album: churches
salmon, turquoise and gold
cooling to monochrome.

A woman floating a tablecloth,
spreading it near the steps to the Metro,
laying out knives, forks, three towels,
a smart red skirt, a small glass cat,
a yellow lampshade and a carriage clock.
(Or was it somewhere else I saw the clock?)
Sadness rises from lino,
absence waits in a drawer.

Standing outside Kiev Station,
fifteen women in line,
behind a gauze of falling snow,
heads bound in layered woollen scarfs,
a bottle of vodka in each mittened hand:
they seem to board the dark green trains,
like grannies in a Giles cartoon,
and dwindle for a thousand miles to 1943.

What's left is always
a jigsaw of pottery,
a fretted iron spoon.

Electroplate

Any number of umbrellas and girlfriends,
both parents, a ceramic bowl, swirling
orange and turquoise and biscuit

like the clouds of a gas giant: all gone,
just twinges. What wakes me at four
is knowing that my memory's wired to a cathode,

that a thin, incessant rain of words
falls on my past, that I can't,
for example, remember, for the life of me,

how it felt when Masha pulled on her boots
in the foyer of the Novaya Opera
(the shape of her smile, the curve of her back)

because what's taken its place is my poem,
the moment's epitaph and tombstone:
'She smiles as, slowly, she zips them'.

The thick-fleshed roach I've landed down the years
which thumped on the bank and whiplashed in my hands
have turned into tinplated knick-knacks.

Two Rivers Press has been publishing in and about Reading since 1994.
Founded by the artist Peter Hay (1951–2003), the press continues
to delight readers, local and further afield, with its varied list of
individually designed, thought-provoking books.